SOUPS & STARTERS

SOUPS & STARTERS

SEAFOOD

SEAFOOD

MEAT & POULTRY

MEAT & POULTRY

PASTA &RICE

PASTA & RICE

VEGETABLES
&SALADS

VEGETABLES & SALADS

SWEET
TREATS

Weights & Measurements

Oven Temperatures

100°C	very slow	200°F	Gas Mark 1
120°C	very slow	250°F	Gas Mark 1
150°C	slow	300°F	Gas Mark 2
165°C	warm	325°F	Gas Mark 2–3
180°C	moderate	350°F	Gas Mark 4
190°C	moderately hot	375°F	Gas Mark 5
200°C	moderately hot	400°F	Gas Mark 6
220°C	hot	420°F	Gas Mark 7
230°C	very hot	450°F	Gas Mark 8
250°C	very hot	485°F	Gas Mark 9

Solid Measures

Metric	Imperial
10 g	⅓ oz
15 g	½ oz
20 g	⅔ oz
30 g	1 oz
45 g	1½ oz
60 g	2 oz
100 g	3½ oz
125 g	4 oz
150 g	5 oz
165 g	5½ oz
180 g	6 oz
200 g	6½ oz
250 g	8 oz
300 g	10 oz
350 g	11½ oz
400 g	13 oz
500 g	1 lb
750 g	1½ lb
1 kg	2 lb

Fluid Measures

Metric	Imperial	Standard Cups
5 ml		1 teaspoon
20 ml	1 fl oz	1 tablespoon
15 ml		1 tablespoon (NZ and US)
50 ml	1¾ fl oz	
60 ml	2 fl oz	¼ cup
80 ml	2¾ fl oz	⅓ cup
100 ml	3½ fl oz	
125 ml	4 fl oz	½ cup
250 ml	8 fl oz	1 cup
500 ml	16 fl oz	2 cups
750 ml	24 fl oz	3 cups
1 L	32 fl oz	4 cups

10 9 8 7 6 5 4 3 2 1

Publisher: Fiona Schultz
Designer: Tania Gomes
Production Manager: Olga Dementiev
Printer: SNP/Leefung Printing Co. Ltd. (China)

Cover photographs by Getty Images
Internal photographs by NHIL

www.newholland.com.au
www.younmgreed.com.au

Fluid Measures

Metric	Imperial	Standard Cups
5 ml		1 teaspoon
20 ml	1 fl oz	1 tablespoon
15 ml		1 tablespoon (NZ and US)
50 ml	1¾ fl oz	
60 ml	2 fl oz	¼ cup
80 ml	2¾ fl oz	⅓ cup
100 ml	3½ fl oz	
125 ml	4 fl oz	½ cup
250 ml	8 fl oz	1 cup
500 ml	16 fl oz	2 cups
750 ml	24 fl oz	3 cups
1 L	32 fl oz	4 cups

10 9 8 7 6 5 4 3 2 1

Publisher: Fiona Schultz
Designer: Tania Gomes
Production Manager: Olga Dementiev
Printer: SNP/Leefung Printing Co. Ltd. (China)

Cover photographs by Getty Images
Internal photographs by NHIL

www.newholland.com.au
www.younmgreed.com.au